D1249535

All-Star Players™

MEET DIRK NOWITZKI

Basketball's Blond Bomber

Sloan MacR

PowerKiDS press
New York

Published in 2009 by The Rosen Publishing Group, Inc.
29 East 21st Street, New York, NY 10010

First Edition

Editor: Amelie von Zumbusch
Book Design: Greg Tucker
Photo Researcher: Jessica Gerweck

Photo Credits: Cover, pp. 4, 11, 12, 16, 18, 19, 22, 25, 29, 30 © Getty Images; p. 7 © AFP/Getty Images; p. 8 © www.iStockphoto.com/Andrew Chambers; p. 10 © Bongarts/Getty Images; pp. 14, 15, 20, 23, 26, 27 © NBAE/Getty Images.

Library of Congress Cataloging-in-Publication Data

MacRae, Sloan.
Meet Dirk Nowitzki : basketball's blond bomber / Sloan MacRae. — 1st ed.
p. cm. — (All-star players)
Includes index.
ISBN 978-1-4358-2709-7 (library binding) — ISBN 978-1-4358-3101-8 (pbk.)
ISBN 978-1-4358-3107-0 (6-pack)
1. Nowitzki, Dirk, 1978– —Juvenile literature. 2. Basketball players—United States—Biography—Juvenile literature. I. Title.
GV884.N69 M33 2009
796.323092—dc22
[B]

2008024394

Manufactured in the United States of America

Contents

Dirk Nowitzki generally plays power forward, but he has played other positions, such as center and small forward, in the past.

Seven Feet and Lots of Baskets

Dirk Nowitzki is an **international** basketball star. Nowitzki is a power forward for the Dallas Mavericks, in the National Basketball Association, or NBA. Nowitzki plays for an American team, but he is not from the United States. He was born in Germany and is still a German citizen.

Most power forwards are good at **defense** and getting **rebounds**. Nowitzki's height makes him more **versatile** than the average power forward. He is 7 feet (2.1 m) tall! It takes more than height to become a star, though. Nowitzki is at the top of the NBA because he worked hard to get there.

All-Star Facts

Nowitzki is an excellent free-throw shooter. Nowitzki says his secret for making free throws is that he sings David Hasselhoff songs in his head. Hasselhoff is a major pop star in Germany.

Nowitzki was born on June 19, 1978, in the German city of Würzburg. Dirk was not the only **athlete** in his family. The entire Nowitzki household loved playing sports. Nowitzki's father was one of the most famous handball players in Germany. His mother, Helga, was a professional basketball player. Dirk's older sister, Silke, was a track star.

Dirk Nowitzki did not start playing basketball until he was about 13 years old. Young Dirk loved playing handball and tennis, too, but he knew that his height could make a difference on the basketball court. He decided to **concentrate** on basketball, and before long he was a local star.

Nowitzki has gone on to play for the German national team. In 2002, he led the German team to win the bronze medal, or third place, at the FIBA World Championship.

14
CROATIA
14

Würzburg, the town where Dirk Nowitzki was born and grew up, is home to a huge palace, a castle, and several beautiful, old churches.

Basketball is not nearly as popular in Germany as it is in the United States. The top German athletes usually pick other sports to play. Nowitzki knew that he could be one of the best basketball players in Germany, but he decided to aim higher. Could he be one of the best in the world? It would take lots of practice and hard work.

"The Boy Is a Genius"

Nowitzki had to take a break from basketball in 1997 and 1998 to serve in the military. German law says that all citizens must serve their country for at least nine months. The time away did not make the teenager rusty, though. He got back on the court and quickly became one of the top players in the country.

When he was only 19, the magazine *BASKET* named Nowitzki German Basketballer of the Year. Nowitzki participated in Nike's Hoop Heroes tour in the same year. The tour was an international event that allowed NBA stars to travel the world and play basketball stars from different countries. The great

All-Star Facts

Nowitzki joined the German team DJK Würzburg in 1994. He got offers to play for other teams as a teenager, but he wanted to stay in Germany to finish his schooling.

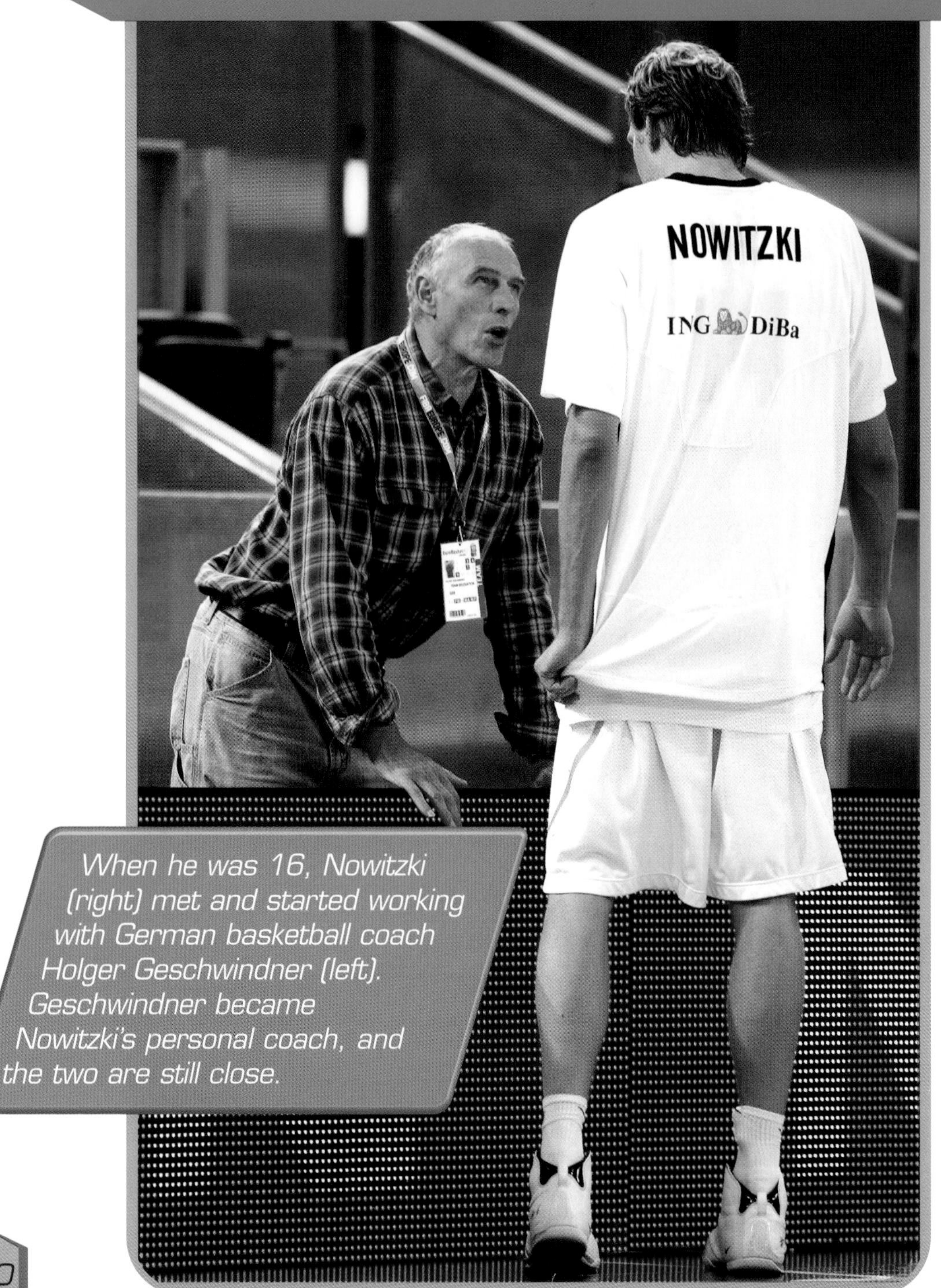

When he was 16, Nowitzki (right) met and started working with German basketball coach Holger Geschwindner (left). Geschwindner became Nowitzki's personal coach, and the two are still close.

Charles Barkley was one of the American stars on the tour. Nowitzki slam-dunked on Barkley. After the game, Barkley said, "The boy is a genius. If he wants to enter the NBA, he can call me." Nowitzki was ready to **compete** against the best basketball players in the world.

Charles Barkley was one of the greatest players in the history of the NBA. During his long career, Barkley played for the Philadelphia 76ers, the Phoenix Suns, and the Houston Rockets.

DALLAS
41

A New Team and a New Friend

Nowitzki decided to enter the 1998 NBA **Draft**. The NBA draft is different from the drafts of other major sports leagues. It works like a **lottery**, and luck plays a very big part. Team representatives pick balls out of a machine. The balls are printed with numbers. Those numbers decide the order in which teams will pick players in the draft.

The Boston Celtics and the Dallas Mavericks both wanted to pick Nowitzki. Celtics coach Rick Pitino said that Nowitzki reminded him of basketball **legend** Larry Bird. The Celtics drew a better number than the Mavericks, so the Celtics had an earlier turn. It looked like Nowitzki was headed to Boston. However, the Celtics never had the chance to pick him. The Milwaukee Bucks had

Nowitzki was picked ninth in the first round of the 1998 NBA Draft.

On June 29, 1998, Nowitzki appeared at a Dallas Mavericks press conference, or meeting with reporters, so that Mavericks fans could learn more about their team's newest player.

an even earlier turn. They picked Nowitzki and quickly traded him to the Mavericks.

The Mavericks needed all the help they could get. When Nowitzki joined the Mavericks for the 1998–1999 season, the team had not made the **play-offs** for nine years. Nowitzki was not the only talented new player on the Mavericks that season.

Point guard Steve Nash joined the Mavericks from the Phoenix Suns. Nowitzki and Nash had a lot in common. They were both new to Dallas and did not know very many people. They became best friends.

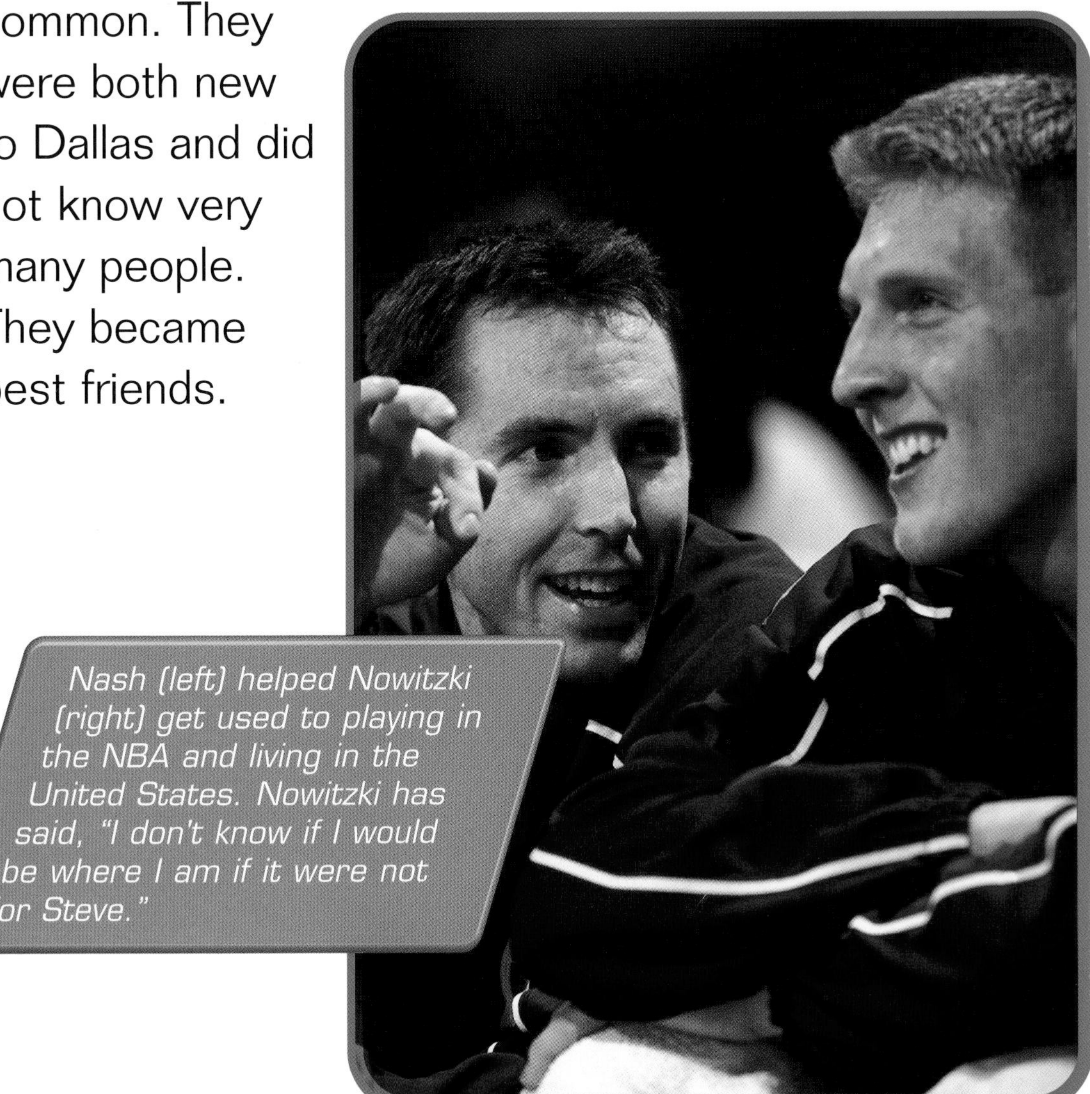

Nash (left) helped Nowitzki (right) get used to playing in the NBA and living in the United States. Nowitzki has said, "I don't know if I would be where I am if it were not for Steve."

MAVERICKS
41

The Dallas Mavericks

Nowitzki's first season in Dallas was rough. There was an argument between the NBA and the players about their pay. No games could be played until both sides agreed. The argument was settled in February 1999, but the season was cut short.

When Nowitzki finally got a chance to play, he did not play well. The NBA was more competitive than German basketball. Dallas fans began to boo him. It would have been easy for Nowitzki to give up and return home. He could always be a top player in Germany. However, Nowitzki did not do that. He decided to train for the next season.

Nowitzki's hard work paid off. He played in every game of the 1999–2000 season and was the runner-up for the NBA Most Improved Player

Nowitzki became a much stronger player during the 1999–2000 season. He averaged 17.5 points per game, up from 8.2 points per game the season before.

Nowitzki was the Mavericks' top scorer in the 2000–2001 season. He scored a total of 1,784 points over the course of the season!

Award. In 2001, he became the second player in NBA history to score more than 100 three-pointers and make more than 100 blocks in one season.

That same year, Nowitzki was also the first Maverick ever to make the All-NBA team. Only the very best players at each position form the All-NBA Team. Nowitzki and Nash had transformed the Mavericks into one of the better teams in the league. In 2001, Dallas made the play-offs for the first time in 11 years! Fans no longer booed Nowitzki. He was one of the NBA's **elite**.

Though he is best known as a great shooter, Nowitzki has worked hard to become a better defensive player, too.

41
TORONTO
44
TORONTO
TORONTO
8
TXU
TXU

Nowitzki played his best season yet in 2001–2002. He had 13 games with at least 30 points and at least 10 rebounds. Only two other players in the NBA played better that year. The Mavericks made the play-offs again, and they **swept** the Minnesota Timberwolves in the first round. Unfortunately, the Mavericks fell in the next round to the Sacramento Kings.

Nowitzki became the Mavericks' franchise player. This means that the team's managers built their entire team around Nowitzki with players who could **complement** his skills. Unfortunately, it also meant that Nash left the Mavericks and returned to the Phoenix Suns in 2004.

In 2006, Nowitzki led the Mavericks to the NBA Finals. The team lost to the Miami Heat, but

By the early 2000s, Nowitzki had become known as one of the most powerful players in the NBA.

Nowitzki was proud to help his team reach its first finals appearance. Nowitzki and the Mavericks returned with 67 victories and the best record of the 2006–2007 regular season. Only five teams in NBA history had ever won

Though the Mavericks lost the 2006 NBA Finals, Nowitzki played well and led his team to win the first two games of the series.

more games in the regular season. Basketball **experts** and **journalists** voted Nowitzki the 2006–2007 Most Valuable Player, or MVP. This means he did more for his team than any other player in the NBA. He was the first European ever to win the award. Nowitzki had become one of the best basketball players in the world.

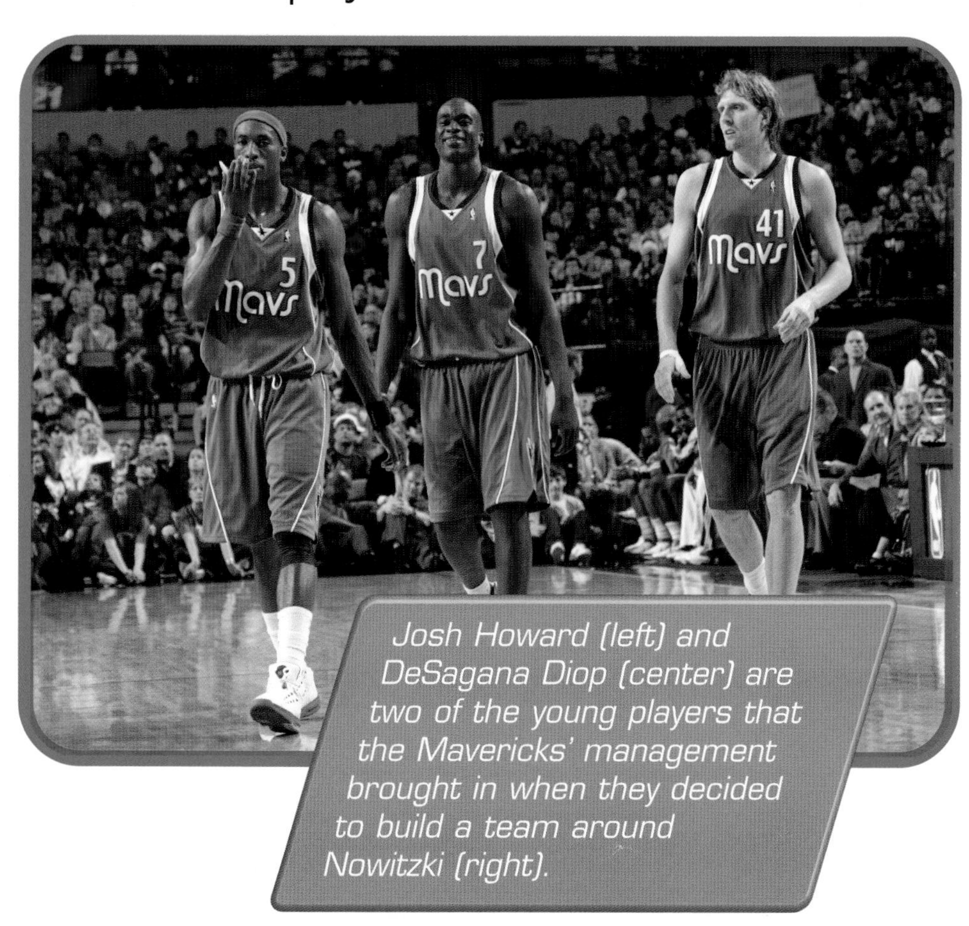

Josh Howard (left) and DeSagana Diop (center) are two of the young players that the Mavericks' management brought in when they decided to build a team around Nowitzki (right).

Not All Basketball

When the NBA season is over, Nowitzki plays on Germany's team in FIBA. FIBA is the international basketball league. Nowitzki helped Germany win the bronze medal, or third place, in the 2002 World Basketball Championship.

However, Nowitzki's life is not all basketball. A coach once told him that it is important for a person to be good at more than just one thing. Nowitzki listened to his coach and learned to play music. He still plays the saxophone and the guitar in his spare time. Nash no longer plays for the Mavericks, but he and Nowitzki remain great friends. In fact, Nowitzki became the godfather of Nash's twin daughters.

All-Star Facts

Nowitzki appeared briefly in the basketball movie *Like Mike*.

Even though he is a huge basketball star, Dirk Nowitzki is a shy and private person.

Here, Nowitzki (right) is receiving an award from the Make-A-Wish Foundation, a group that supports children who are sick.

Nowitzki likes to help people. He created his own charity called the Dirk Nowitzki Foundation. The foundation raises money to help poor and sick children all over the world. It also provides grants to many children's organizations. Some of the grants include money to build playgrounds for children in poor neighborhoods, to provide care for children in homeless shelters, and to buy books and backpacks for children in poor families. Nowitzki's mother and sister help him run the foundation. Nowitzki also buys toys to give to children in Dallas hospitals during the holiday season. In 2007, he won the NBA Community Assist Award for helping others.

Dirk Nowitzki supports a number of groups that work to make the world a better place for kids. Here, he is signing autographs, or copies of his name, for a group of young fans.

Hard Work Pays Off

It is true that Dirk Nowitzki's size helps him be a great basketball player. However, there are a lot of tall people in the world. Most of them are not NBA superstars. Nowitzki climbed to the top of the NBA because he works hard. He knows that he can always get better.

Nowitzki is such a good player that the NBA now looks at other European basketball players. He opened the door for other stars, such as France's Tony Parker. Fans around the world cheer for Nowitzki in German, in English, and in many other languages. He works hard so he will not let his fans down.

All-Star Facts

On March 8, 2008, Nowitzki became the Mavericks' all-time scoring leader with 16,644 points.

As of 2008, Nowitzki holds the Mavericks' team records for points scored, rebounds, three-pointers, and free throws.

Stat Sheet

Height: 7' (2.1 m)
Weight: 245 pounds (111 kg)
Team: Dallas Mavericks
Position: Forward
Uniform Number: 41
Date of Birth: June 19, 1978

2007–2008 Season Stats

Games Played	3-Point Percentage	Free-Throw Percentage	Rebounds per Game	Assists per Game	Points per Game
77	.359	.879	8.6	3.5	23.6

NBA Career Stats as of Summer 2008

Games Played	3-Point Percentage	Free-Throw Percentage	Rebounds per Game	Assists per Game	Points per Game
758	.379	.870	8.6	2.7	22.4

Glossary

athlete (ATH-leet) Someone who takes part in sports.
compete (kum-PEET) To oppose another in a game or test.
complement (KOM-pleh-ment) To work well with.
concentrate (KON-sen-trayt) To direct one's thoughts and attention to one thing.
defense (DEE-fents) When a team tries to stop the other team from scoring.
draft (DRAFT) The selection of people for a special purpose.
elite (ay-LEET) A small, powerful group.
experts (EK-sperts) People who know a lot about a subject.
international (in-tur-NA-shuh-nul) Having to do with more than one country.
journalists (JER-nul-ists) People who gather and write news for newspapers or magazines.
legend (LEH-jend) A person who has been famous and honored for a very long time.
lottery (LAH-tuh-ree) The drawing of counters, called lots, used to decide something.
play-offs (PLAY-ofs) Games played after the regular season ends to see who will play in the championship game.
point guard (POYNT GAHRD) A basketball player who directs his or her team's forward plays on the court.
rebounds (REE-bowndz) Times when a person gets control of the ball after a missed shot.
swept (SWEPT) Won all stages of a game or contest.
versatile (VER-suh-tul) Able to do many different things well.

Index

Web Sites

Due to the changing nature of Internet links, PowerKids Press has developed an online list of Web sites related to the subject of this book. This site is updated regularly. Please use this link to access the list:
www.powerkidslinks.com/asp/dirkn/